This Book Belor

· ·

we hope you enjoy this book, and we would really appreciate your feedback/review on Amazon to help support us so we can keep creating more books!

A note to parents

There are many ways to teach the alphabet, and what works best may vary depending on the child and their learning style. Some effective methods include:

- Reading books: Reading alphabet books (like this one) can help children to see the letters in context and make them more meaningful for them.
- Singing the alphabet song: The alphabet song is a catchy tune that helps children to remember the sequence of letters in the alphabet.

- Using hands-on activities: Children learn best when they can see, touch, and experience something themselves. So you can use hands-on activities such as puzzles, blocks, or play-doh to form the letters.
- Using technology: There are many educational apps and websites available that can make learning the alphabet fun and interactive for children.
- Using flashcards: Write each letter on a flashcard and have the child say the name and the sound of the letter while showing them the flashcard.

Ultimately, it's important to be patient and make learning the alphabet fun for the child.

Benefits of rhyming

Rhyming can have many benefits for children when it comes to language development. Some of these benefits include:

- Enhancing phonological awareness: Rhyming helps children to become more aware of the sounds in words, which is an important skill for reading and spelling.
- Improving vocabulary: When children hear and learn new words through rhyming, they are expanding their vocabulary.
- Encouraging creativity: Rhyming can inspire children to come up with their own words and phrases, promoting creativity and imagination.

- Building listening skills: Listening to rhymes helps children to tune in to the sounds around them and improves their listening skills.
- Making learning fun: Rhyming can make learning fun and engaging, making it more likely that children will retain the information they learn.
- Preparing for reading: Understanding and recognizing rhymes is a key pre-reading skill, as it helps children to identify patterns in words and predict what might come next.

Ultimately, rhyming can be a powerful tool for language development, as it helps children to learn new words.

Best age to start teaching the alphabet

It's recommended to start teaching the alphabet to children around the age of 2 or 3 years old. This is the age when children start to develop an interest in letters and sounds, and when their cognitive and language skills are developing rapidly. However, every child is different and some may show an interest in letters and numbers before that age.

Teaching the alphabet is not a one-time event, but rather a process that will continue throughout the child's education. At first, children will learn the names and shapes of the letters, then the sounds that they make, and eventually how to connect them to form words.

Teaching the alphabet with rhymes

Teaching the alphabet as letters and words and using them in rhymes can be particularly beneficial for children because it helps to make the learning process more interactive, memorable, and fun.

In case you want to track progress or just write some notes (or just doodle!), we have included some lined paper at the end of this book.

We certainly hope you and your child/children enjoy this book!

A is for Alligator

alligator

Anthony the alligator, swam
in the swamp,
with a big grin, and a tail
that thump,
He caught his prey, with a
quick snap,
And lounged in the sun,
taking a nap.

B is for Beaver

B
beaver

Borris the beaver, with his
flat tail,
Built his home, without fail,
He chewed on wood, with his
strong jaws,
To make a home, that never
falls.

c is for CAT

Kat the cat, with her soft
fur,
Loved to nap, in a cozy
purr,
She'd stretch and yawn,
with a playful grin,
Then chase a ball, or a toy
on a spin.

D is for Donkey

D
donkey

Doug the donkey, with his strong back,
Loved to roam, on a dirt track.
He was hardworking, and never shy,
He'd bray and bray, as he trotted by.

E is for elephant

E

elephant

Ellie the elephant, big and
grand,
with her trunk held high, she
roamed the land,
when she trumpeted loud,
with a mighty sound,
And all the animals would
gather around.

F is for Frog

F
frog

Freddie the frog, with his
big leap,
Jumped high and far,
without a peep,
He croaked and croaked, in
the pond,
and with his friends, he sang
a song.

G is for Giraffe

G
giraffe

Gayle the giraffe, with her spots so bright,
stood tall and proud, a graceful sight.
she nibbled on leaves, from the tallest trees,
And gazed out far, with the softest breeze.

H is for Horse

H
horse

Henry the horse, with his
shiny mane,
Galloped through the fields,
without a rein,
He was free and wild, with a
heart full of grace,
A beautiful sight, in any
place.

I is for Iguana

I

iguana

Ian the iguana, with his long tail,
climbed the trees, without fail,
He basked in the sun, and loved to hide,
watching the world, from the treetop side.

J is for Jellyfish

jellyfish

June the jellyfish, with her transparent bell,
Drifted in the ocean, like a floating shell.
She swayed and swirled, with the ocean's flow,
A graceful creature, with a beauty that glows.

k is for kangaroo

K
kangaroo

Kylie the baby kangaroo,
with her little hop, bounced
around, with a playful plop,
she kicked her legs, and
wiggled her ears,
exploring the world, with a
heart full of cheers.

L is for Lion

L

lion

Leo the lion, with his mighty
roar,
Ruled the savannah, forever
more,
He was the king afterall, of
the jungle land,
with a powerful roar, that
shook the sand.

M is for Mouse

M
mouse

mia the mouse, with her small size,
sneaked around, with stealth and guise,
she scurried about, with her tiny feet,
gathering crumbs, and finding a treat to eat.

N is for Numbat

N
numbat

Norman the numbat, with
fur so sleek
Ran through the bush, with
nimble feet
He munched on termites,
with great delight
Living his life, in the morning
light.

o is for octopus

octopus

ollie the octopus, with
tentacles eight
slithered and slipped,
through the ocean so great
He changed colors, to blend
in with the sea
And caught fish, for his
dinner with wonderous glee.

P is for panda

P
panda

Amanda the panda, with fur
so black and white
Loved to eat bamboo, from
morning to night
she climbed through the
trees, with grace and ease
And took long naps, under
the bamboo trees.

q is for quetzal

Q

quetzal

Queenie the quetzal, with
feathers so bright
Fluttered and flew, in the
forest so light
She danced in the branches,
with beauty and pride
And sang her sweet song,
with her head held high.

R is for Raccoon

R
raccoon

Ralph the raccoon, with a
bushy tail so grand
Loved to explore, in the
forest and on land
He found tasty treats, in
the dark of the night
And stored them away, till
everything was just right.

s is for sheep

S

sheep

sarah the sheep, with wool so fluffy and white
Loved to graze, on the green fields in sight
she followed the flock, all day long
And baa-ed her way, into a peaceful song.

T is for Turtle

T

turtle

Tommy the turtle, with a
shell so neat
Moved slow and steady, with
purpose and fleet
He explored the pond, with
curiosity
And basked in the sun, in
total tranquility.

U is for unicorn

U

unicorn

una the unicorn, with a horn
so bright
galloped through the
meadow, with all her might
she sparkled and shone, in
the sun's golden rays
And spread magic and
wonder, in all her ways.

v is for viper

viper

victor the viper, with
scales so sleek
slid through the grass, with
a hiss so unique
He hunted for mice, with his
venomous bite
But feared by all, he lived a
lonely life.

w is for whale

W

whale

willow the whale, with a tail
so grand
swam in the ocean, with a
pod in hand
she sang her song, that
echoed far and wide
And leaped out of water,
with a joyful glide.

x is for x-ray fish

x- ray fish

xander the x-ray fish, with
bones so see-through
swam in the coral, with a
flash of light blue
He darted and dodged,
through the reef with ease
And amazed all the other
fish, with his x-ray breeze.

Y is for yak

yak

Yara the Yak, with fur so
thick and warm
Roamed the mountains, with
her herd in a swarm
she munched on grass, and
moss from the rocks
And braved the cold, with
her fluffy yak locks.

z is for zebra

Z
zebra

zak the zebra, with stripes
so bold
galloped through the
savannah, with young and
old
He blended in the herd, with
his camouflage
And outran the lions, with a
quick swift dodge.

My Notes

_____

_____

_____

_____

_____

_____

_____

_____

My Notes

My Notes

_____

_____

_____

_____

_____

_____

_____

_____

My Notes

_____

_____

_____

_____

_____

_____

_____

_____

My Notes

_____

_____

_____

_____

_____

_____

_____

_____

My Notes

_____

_____

_____

_____

_____

_____

_____

_____

My Notes

_____

_____

_____

_____

_____

_____

_____

_____

My Notes

_____

_____

_____

_____

_____

_____

_____

_____

My Notes

_____

_____

_____

_____

_____

_____

_____

_____

Printed in Great Britain
by Amazon

37689379R00044